W9-BSW-984

Health Communications, Inc.
Deerfield Beach, Florida

Jessamine County Public Library
600 South Main Street
Nicholasville, KY 40356
859-885-3523

cibooks.com

Library of Congress Cataloging-in-Publication Data
is available through the Library of Congress

© 2019 Erin Merryn

ISBN-13: 978-07573-2184-9 (Hardcover)
ISBN-10: 07573-2184-4 (Hardcover)
ISBN-13: 978-07573-2185-6 (ePub)
ISBN-10: 07573-2185-2 (ePub)

All rights reserved. Printed in the United States of America. No part of this publication may be reproduced, stored in a retrieval system or transmitted in any form or by any means, electronic, mechanical, photocopying, recording or otherwise without the written permission of the publisher.

HCI, its Logos and Marks are trademarks of Health Communications, Inc.

Publisher: Health Communications, Inc.
            3201 S.W. 15th Street
            Deerfield Beach, FL 33442–8190

Cover and inside designs by Larissa Hise Henoch
Inside book formatting by Lawna Patterson Oldfield

Once in a great while, a pet enters our lives, enchants us, and changes everything. A giant soul inside of a tiny creature who most assuredly was sent to us for reasons beyond our understanding. Bailey, a tiny orange tabby cat, broke the mold when he became Erin Merryn's furry companion hailing back from her college days when he illegally shared her

dorm room through to becoming the eldest sibling to her three young daughters. What went on in Erin's household morphed into a career for Bailey as family entertainer and social media mega-star. His behavior was beyond cat-like with monk-like tolerance and uncharacteristic patience. Most cats would never be caught in a tuxedo or wearing sunglasses or sitting in a high chair to eat dinner, but that's what made him Bailey, No Ordinary Cat.

Bailey leapt into my heart (literally) the day I went to a pet store to pass some time. I'd never met such an affectionate cat. I couldn't leave without him. He was my copilot, my fur baby, my daily dose of laughter.

The tear-jerking part of the story is that Bailey, like all cats, was not destined to live forever. A heart-break to his human siblings, Bailey was summoned to kitty heaven after some struggles with his health at the ripe old age of fourteen. He gave the family a bonus year when he was first diagnosed but his nine lives ended before he could enjoy being heralded as a bestselling book star. But, at the time of writing this note, the late Bailey still enjoys off-the-charts social media fame and has been the subject of stories as far as Taiwan and Australia. The outpouring of love for this extraordinary animal has come from all over the world in letters, gifts, and a plethora of stuffed orange kitties for the children (Abby, Hannah, and Claire Joy). Never mind the "You Are My Sunshine" video that virally made it on *Ellen* and *Good Morning America* and countless blogs while Bailey was still alive. Rarely is there a dry eye at the end of this video!

Turn the pages and we guarantee mostly laughter, some expressions of disbelief, and possibly a tear or two when you witness the many expressions of Bailey's personality and his one-in-a-million spirit. We know you'll appreciate this lovable rascal who will continue to evoke warm feelings, smiles, and love beyond his years here on earth.

Now, without further ado, we give you, Bailey, No Ordinary Cat.

Naps
and
cuddling,
my two favorite things.

Yes, I know

I clean up well.

She is my
sunshine.

Would you please

stop
laughing

and just unwrap me already?

Does this
onesie make me
look fat?

I am the

teacher's

pet…

literally.

Hey, put your
phone down and

look at
me!

Are you sure

you know what you're doing?
You look a bit young for
med school.

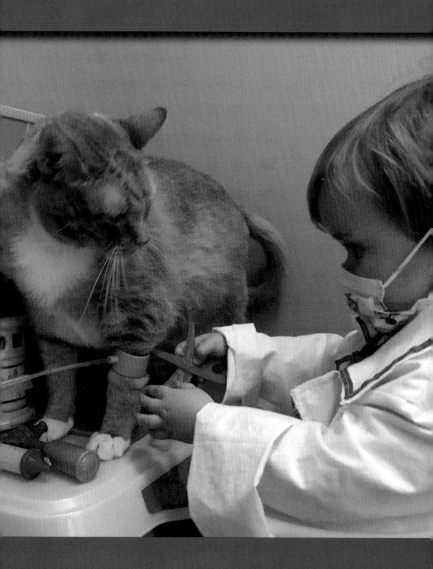

And they **call this** "some assembly required"?

What, you have
never seen a cat

potty-train

a toddler before?

Cats

need

vacations,

too.

I said I wanted a

Cat-illac

and they got me
this Mustang.

Is it my imagination,
or do these pillows keep
kicking me?

28

When is someone going
to tell them that

cats hate
water?

The things I do for
love.

I think we're
going to need a
bigger tub.

34

I'm the
cutest bug
in the bunch.

She's

mine.

I was here

first.

I told you

not

to wake her.

She must be

getting back

at me for nine months
of laying on her in
Mama's belly.

Yes, I know I'm

cute.

When will they
figure out
I'm a boy?

Sometimes the
best gifts
aren't wrapped.

If I sleep,
she will sleep;
it works like a charm.

Sometimes
you just have to
roll with it.

You know,
I really don't think

anyone

else is paying attention.

Hold on, Mom.
Just gotta update the
fans.

Naptime.

You act all tough now,
but just wait
until I get this
door open!

You are getting sleepy.
No, wait,
I am getting sleepy.

This is how you get on

Mom's good side.

They say every vote

counts.

Don't tell anyone
but I'm her
favorite.

Apparently I need to
eat all of
my vegetables.

I don't think
the chef

read my
bib.

Finally,
my turn!

Who says cats are

finicky

eaters?

Better than

the Elf on the Shelf,
the Cat on the Carpet.

Aren't there
supposed
to be presents
under there?

Enjoying my

cat-ppuccino.

My other crimes include impersonating humans and

stealing hearts.

BAD PET

CHARGE:

IDENTITY
THEFT

Just call me
Pablo
Pi-cat-sso.

Kisses.

More Kisses.

Where are all the kids?
I bought

Kit-Cats

and 3 Mouse-keteers.

94

No one talk to
me until I've had

my coffee.

Baby Claire
thinks this book is a real
snoozer.

Hug

like you mean it.

So let me understand,
this product was

not tested

on an animal but it is
now being worn
by an animal.

I'm ready

for my close-up.
The baby not so much.

Did somebody say
birthday?

I wish for a new toy mouse
and a big pile of

catnip.

Is there any chance
that there's a little

brother

in there?

They say
good things
come to those who wait.

Why does she get the
cute hat?

Who says cats
can't read?

116

Is it just me

or are my friends
a little "stuffy"?

All I need
is red, white…

and you.

It's rare

to find a cat who makes house calls.

…in case you

haven't

figured it out yet.